HAND OVER HEART

Poems 1981-1988

David Trinidad

AMETHYST PRESS
NEW YORK, NEW YORK

Published in the United States of America by Amethyst Press, Inc.,
Six West Thirty-Second Street, Penthouse, New York, New York
10001-3808.

COVER ART BY JIM ISERMANN

Grateful acknowledgement is made to the editors of the following
publications, in which certain of the poems in this book originally
appeared: *American Poetry Since 1970: Up Late* (Four Walls Eight
Windows, 1987), *Barney, B City, Brooklyn Review, Columbia, CUZ,
enclitic, In Touch, The Jacaranda Review, The L.A.I.C.A. Journal,
L.A. Weekly,* Beyond Baroque's *Magazine, Male Review, Mirage, No
Apologies, OINK!, Out of This World: An Anthology of Writing from
St. Mark's Poetry Project* (Crown, 1991), *The Paris Review, Poetry
Loves Poetry: An Anthology of Los Angeles Poets* (Momentum Press,
1985), *Santa Monica Review, Shiny International, Snap, St. Mark's
Poetry Project Newsletter,* and *Under 35: The New Generation of
American Poets* (Anchor Books, 1989).

Some of these poems also appeared in the following chapbooks:
Living Doll (Illuminati, 1986), *Monday, Monday* (Cold Calm Press,
1985), *November* (Hanuman Books, 1987), and *Three Stories*
(Hanuman Books, 1988).

For their friendship and support, I would like to thank Dennis
Cooper, Tim Dlugos, Bob Flanagan, Raymond Foye, Christopher
Harrity, John E. Kralick, Sheree Levin, Kathleen Lorenzen, Eileen
Myles, Helen Rosenstock, James Schuyler, Michael Silverblatt,
Roy Smith, and members of the anonymous fellowship. I would
also like to thank Ira Silverberg for his help at home.

Trinidad, David, 1953-
   Hand over heart : poems 1981-1988 / David Trinidad.
     p. cm.
   ISBN 0-927200-07-4 : $9.95
   1. Gay men—Poetry. I. Title.
   PS3570.R53H36 1991   90-28519
   811'.54—dc20   CIP

for Amy Gerstler

CONTENTS

V

VI

VII

I

ORDINARY THINGS

On the patio, next
to a large, rather
awkwardly transplanted
bromeliad, sits
the blackened hibachi
that hasn't been used
since last summer
when a number
of us, who knew you
intimately, got to-
gether to commemorate
the first anniversary
of your death.

It wasn't much
of an afternoon.
For the most part
I was quiet, kept
myself preoccupied
while everyone ate
and talked about
ordinary (it seemed
to me) things.
Your name came up
once or twice—
I can't remember
in what context.
No one cried.

After we hugged
and kissed each other
good-bye, I rinsed
the glasses and plates
and placed them
in the dishwasher. I
sat down and listened
to music (your
records—they were
all scratched).
I chain-smoked and
drank until I was
numb enough to fall
asleep without

reexperiencing
that impact—
one set of headlights
abruptly intercepted
by another, the unut-
terable welding of
metal to flesh—
instant blackness.

This year it
is different.
Everyone is off
doing the things
students usually
do after graduating
from college:
marrying, starting
families, making
lots of money at
jobs you would
have thought out
of character for
your friends—
such a *gifted* group.

I light a cigarette,
sip at this scotch.
In it, there is one
small ice cube left.
It is still warm out-
side, although it
is getting late.
It is very quiet and
the light is faint.

WINDOW SEAT

How much closer are we to the moon?
Tonight it's a mere crescent in
an altogether black sky somewhere
over Kansas, or so the voice of our
captain assures us. I've already
forgotten how many thousands of feet
he said we're flying at. I've also
forgotten how many cocktails the iden-
tical blonde stewardesses have brought
me. I feel, well, like a crossword
puzzle: 5 down, an alcoholic beverage
served on airplanes in tiny bottles,
begins with S-C-O. Back in New York
City, the boys are undoubtedly flir-
ting with the boys at the Boy Bar.
How I wish I were still there, wide-
eyed and excited, in that flurry of
good-looks. Up here, in the section
where smoking's permitted, I'm fin-
gering an empty matchbook and a few
leftover subway tokens. They're as
useless now as the valium I took
on the bus to the airport. Most of my
fellow passengers, however, have nodded
off. Others rented headsets, muf-
fling the purity of the soundless film
on the small screen, a romantic comedy
I observe with little interest until
sudden turbulence signals a familiar
"plink" and FASTEN SEATBELT lights up
overhead. My eyelids are leaden; I'm
too tired to obey. What time is it
on the coast this flight is speeding
toward, enabling me to regain the
three hours I willfully abandoned
last week? But what would I have done
with them then, except sleep and dream?

DREAMS

At the stroke of midnight, we
sat down on a queen-size bed
to watch a special screening
of *The Lost Weekend* on TV.
A previously censored scene
(in which Ray Milland, drunk
out of his mind on Irish whis-
key, tries on Jane Wyman's
stylish leopard coat in front
of a full-length mirror) had
been restored to the film.
I felt privileged to see it.
The bed tilted a little and
I realized it was resting on
the edge of a steep cliff.
Miles below us, the ocean
glistened. It looked like
sheet metal. The drop made
me so dizzy I was almost sick.
I wanted to warn you of the
great danger we were in, but
you were engrossed in the movie
and I was afraid you might get
mad if you were disturbed.
We were fine until you shifted
your weight. We tipped back-
wards and, on the mattress,
started sliding down the side
of the mountain like those kids
that sailed through the air on
a block of ice in Walt Disney's
In Search of the Castaways.
I panicked and shouted: "My bed!
My comforter!" Then I noticed
the sky: it was a shade of the
most amazing blue. You reached
underneath the pillow and
produced a bottle of amyl
nitrate, which you proceeded
to take off the cap of and
sniff as we kept plummeting.
You passed it to me just when
we were about to hit the water.

I woke up and looked at the
alarm clock. It was 3:30 a.m.
My heart was pounding. I calmed
down, fell asleep again, and
dreamed that I was sitting at
a picnic table somewhere in
Sequoia National Park. One by
one, I ripped all the pages out
of an old magazine, an issue
of *Time*. The cover looked
familiar (I think I remembered
it from when I was a teenager),
although inside there was
no text, only glossy stills
of silent movie stars. I
didn't recognize any of them.
My grandfather, who had been
standing near a barbecue pit
with the rest of the family,
noticed I was sitting alone
and walked over to the table.
My grandfather had always
frightened me. I looked
up at him, then down at the
torn photographs. Gently, he
placed his hand on my shoulder.
"The stars are silent tonight,"
he said. I wanted to ask
him to forgive me. Instead,
I turned away from him, hating
myself as I did, but I was
afraid I wouldn't be able
to give enough in return
for the presence of that kind
and forever unknowable old man.

GREAT-GRANDMOTHER SMITH

In the two photographs I have of her,
taken over ten years apart, she wears
the same plain dress. In the first,
she sits in the sun (under a parasol)
next to her daughter, Marguerite, my
mother's mother, whose smile is warm,
while Great-grandmother's is stiff
beneath spectacles. Her white hair
is pinned tight. Her figure is slight,
almost skeletal. In the second picture,
she stands alone on the front steps
of the house on W. Montecito Street
in Sierra Madre, where we visited her
when I was a child. I remember little
but details of those infrequent trips:
the dense oleanders that fenced her
yard from the neighbors', a wobbly
stepladder my brother and I reached
for ripe apricots and plums from,
the knee-high weeds we romped through
out back. The small garage was off
limits; in it, black widows guarded
the steamer trunks stuffed with her
memories—porcelain dolls with vacant
faces, petite high-button shoes, and
the padded velvet family album filled
with photographs of her own great-
grandparents, who migrated from France
to Canada in the mid 1800's, and of
her parents before and after they met
in Cambridge Square, married, and
moved to Bristol, Connecticut, where
she was born (the first of twelve
children), brought up, and, at the
age of fifteen, handed to a local
watchmaker turned homesteader, who
with his "drunkard of a brother"
raised gamecocks on Chippens Hill,
a farm notoriously popular in the
area for the cockfights often staged
there. Great-grandmother gave birth
to two sons, grew and sold vegetables
door-to-door in town, transplanted

roots to the dirt floor of the cellar
each fall. But the goings-on in the
barn unsettled her and she objected
until, eight months pregnant with
Marguerite, she warned the two men
that, should the drinking, gambling
and fighting not stop, she would one
by one wring their prize roosters'
necks. The ruckus continued and she
did just that. The following day, her
brother-in-law left for more amiable
parts and her husband returned to his
former trade. Years later, after he
came to California and couldn't find
work, he took up gardening. The family
lived in Sierra Madre, on the opulent
estate of Arthur Gerlach, who once
photographed Einstein and the Ford
brothers, and invested wisely in
Detroit Edison's prosperous stock.
By then, Marguerite had blossomed
into a young beauty, was crowned
"Queen of the Wisteria Vines" in
an annual spring festival, fell
in love with Harlan, Mr. Gerlach's
youngest son, to whom she was wed
in an elaborate ceremony that made
the front page of the city's daily
paper. Their marriage, although it
introduced the Smiths to money and
enabled Great-grandfather to retire
in comfort, ended when my mother
was three—Marguerite left Harlan
as soon as she learned he had lost
everything they owned in a Friday
night poker game. Not long after
the divorce, Harlan died of a burst
appendix and Great-grandfather passed
away in his sleep. He was seventy.
Marguerite got her driver's license,
worked for the telephone company
while Great-grandmother watched after
my mother, waking her early every
Saturday so they could take the Red
Car to Los Angeles, where she'd

rummage through the Goodwill ware-
house and thrift shops on Skid Row
for wool skirts and coats, which
she would lug back in brown paper
bags, split at the seams with razor
blades, picking off the threads,
then soak and wash, steam press,
cut into inch-wide strips that she
folded, stitched together, wound
into balls like yarn, and used to
braid huge oval rugs. That was
before the Second World War, about
the time Marguerite felt the first
symptoms of a disease later diagnosed
as leukemia. The long, drawn out illness
tainted my mother's adolescence, as
did the news that George, her cousin
and childhood companion, was killed
when a Japanese suicide pilot crashed
into his LST landing craft as it
hauled gasoline off Guadalcanal. He
was seventeen. Marguerite was in her
early thirties when she whispered
"George is calling me" moments before
she died. My mother sat at her side,
dampening her skin. She was fourteen.
Great-grandmother lived to be ninety-
three, although we saw less of her
after she had to be moved to a con-
valescent facility where, heavily
sedated, she simply sat and stared
out the window at passing traffic.
I remember being frightened by the
lady in the next bed because she
mumbled strange things. I was not
quite five, but I can still recall
the living room of her house, how
in its spaciousness I kept myself
silent one Sunday afternoon a month
by counting her spools of colored
thread and lifting the lid of the
piano bench to examine stacks of
faded sheet music. I remember there
were photographs of people I didn't
know above the fireplace and that

I stared up at them as I stared
up at Great-grandmother as she sat
for hours working wool into rugs, her
severe expression matched only by
the intensity with which her fingers
steadfastly braided the fabric.

BEFORE MORNING

The telephone rings. For a split
second she panics, can't focus:
in front of her the television
is high-pitched, an indistinct
pattern she'd slept in spite of.
She clutches the remote control
—the screen flickers off. The
telephone rings again. She pushes
herself from the couch, crosses
the living room sucking in breath
like a long drag on one of her
menthol cigarettes, stops, clears
her throat, lifts the receiver
as it starts to ring a third time.
"Hello." Silence. "Hello." The line
goes dead. She hangs up irritated
yet relieved. No, that was weeks
ago; no, weeks before that—the
countless arrangements and sympathy
cards—that she was terrified of
the telephone ringing in the middle
of the night. Terrified of every-
thing, really, although a part
of her felt numb because it had
become familiar—the parking lot,
lobby, elevator and corridors; the
matter-of-fact tone of the nurses
and hospital operators. Terrified
of meeting her daughter's sunken
eyes, of seeing that fluid seep
through a tube toward the needle
sewn into her wrist. Terrified
of the doctor, his warning that
it could spread quickly once he
"opens her up." In the kitchen, she
chases a shot of whiskey with tap
water, then turns off the lamps,
feels her way along the dark
hall, and lies down on the bed
without undressing. Beside her,
her husband snores. The shutters
slice the light from the street
across the walls and ceiling.

She closes her eyes and pictures
her daughter in their backyard,
on an afternoon years before. She
wears a pink dress; her blonde
hair is in braids. Blindfolded,
she waves her arms and takes
little steps toward the other
children who hold hands and dance
in a circle around her. Later,
she unwraps gifts—a bottle of
bubble bath, an aluminum tea
service—then sits at the picnic
table as the lit cake is set in
front of her, her eyes shut tight.
She makes a wish, opens them
wide, and with one swift breath
blows all eight candles out.

II

TIM'S STOLEN SWEATER

Sunlight which seeps through a part
in the drapes illuminates the rumpled
contents of your suitcase: sweaters
and slacks, and some of those short-
sleeved alligator shirts, the kind
that "clones" wear, though they'd make
you look good—healthy and athletic—
unlike most of the men at the crowded
bar where we met. Before we spoke,
I wanted to reach across and touch
your cheekbone, the scar just under
the left one (I couldn't bring myself
to ask how you'd gotten it, so I
imagined a gang fight in your youth
or a steak knife in the hand of
a lover insane with jealousy). You
introduced yourself. I extended my
hand. Then, in your room, our chit-
chat continued until, abruptly, you
asked, "Do you want to kiss me?" It
was a perfect way to get to the point
and I was impressed. "Yes." Our move-
ments cast shadows of flesh barely
lit by the glow of the motel's neon
sign as it flashed on and off. Just
a few hours sleep. Now, slightly hung
over, I erase one or two of the creases
our bodies made in sheets a maid will
change later in the day, after we've
showered and dressed, gone our sep-
arate ways. You're going out for a
newspaper and a six-pack. I watch you
rummage through your suitcase, pull
on a pair of boxer shorts, jeans, and
the sweater you wore last night—
light blue with thin white stripes
around the chest—which is what I
noticed first, from across the bar,
and then, as I moved closer, how
handsome you were, despite your scar.

POEM

That vast dance floor was the empty universe
I presumed mine alone when I was merely eighteen
and utterly accessible to almost any one of many
made handsome only amidst those rotating lights.

POEM

again like never I feel
my fool way dreamed me
and so you know me
heart of that me I leave
foolish always like love

"C'est plus qu'un crime, c'est une faute"

for Amy Gerstler

In the small hours, several rounds
at Le Café, "one of the swankier
spots West L.A.'s nightlife offers":
pink neon and napkins, essence of
scampi and chateaubriand. Seated at
a table against the wall, listen-
ing to the couples on either side
of us chat *en français,* I was
about to comment on the "ambiance"
of the place when, struck by
the looks of a certain redheaded
waiter, you inadvertently spilled
your second strawberry daiquiri.
It seemed everyone turned to
stare at us and you blushed. I'm
afraid I didn't help much, the way
I laughed. I meant to tell you
then, but in the confusion for-
got, how last week, at work, I
found myself attracted to a rather
brawny refrigerator repairman.
He wore a tight white T-shirt,
the tattoo of a chimera half-
visible beneath one of its sleeves.
A chimera is an imaginary monster
made up of incongruous parts. It
is also a frightful or foolish
fancy. I wrote my telephone number
on a small piece of paper and
slipped it in his pocket before
he left. *Why had she acted so
very rashly?* I read this that
night at a drugstore, on the back
cover of a Harlequin Romance, as
I waited in line to buy a pack
of cigarettes. Walking home,
Hollywood Blvd. was abuzz with
tourists and various low-life
types. I reached my street. It
was late, but fireworks were still
being set off from the magicians'

private club at the top of the
hill. I stopped and looked up,
then started to laugh (It had
to be for my benefit!) as half
the night sky briefly flared
into a brilliant shade of red.

POEM

Sometimes it seems the night conspires

to undo me   It hasn't stopped pouring

and I'm trapped inside listening to songs

that inevitably evoke these sentiments

I'm really lost   Hopelessly immersed

in lyrics   "Love is the answer," etc.

SONG

This single by the all-girl group
I worshipped as an adolescent
sounds exactly like it did on
countless summer after-
noons. Those teenage emotions
survive too—so very seriously
thoughtless as ever.

UP & DOWN

It's another Saturday
night and I ain't got
nobody, but I've still
got at least half of
a quarter of a gram of
"my" drug. I've also
got plenty of beer and
Marlboro Lights. And
music! Although I've
got to keep it low, as
last week a very irate
neighbor complained a-
bout the awful noise I'd
apparently been making
and our strict manager
immediately pounded on
my door, demanding that
I comply with the terms
of my lease or face evic-
tion proceedings. Any-
way, right now Siouxsie
is singing the chorus of
one of my favorite songs:

Myriad lights—they said I'd be impressed
Arabian Knights—at your primitive best.

Someone (I don't remem-
ber who) once gave me
this good advice: "You
must learn how to enter-
tain yourself." Well,
I do have music, and
as faint as it is, it's
uplifting.

*

I'm attracted to the accessories
this drug requires: razor blade
and straw (or tightly-rolled dollar
bill) and mirror tiny enough to fit
into a wallet's private compartment—

32

the little kit conveniently tucked
in my back pocket as I discreetly
and repeatedly slip into bathrooms
at poetry readings and parties.

*

The Chiffons were the first
female group I flipped over.
God! I can clearly recall
the exhilaration I experienced
every afternoon one summer
as I pranced about my bedroom,
posing for an imaginary audience
and lip-syncing the lyrics to
"He's So Fine" (the single's
label was Laurie; the title
of the song on the B-side was
"Oh My Lover," which I equally
adored), while below the open
window, Paul, a blond neigh-
borhood boy I had a secret
crush on, urged my older
brother to "Hit a homer!"
and, at the foot of the
stairs, my mother or my
father screamed up at me
to turn it down.

*

A concerned friend, having heard
I've been doing a lot of cocaine
lately, called me up today and warned:
"Now we don't want you hitting
any unnecessary downward spirals."

*

In 1963, as song after song
from *Meet The Supremes* began
to rise to the top of the charts,
my impressionable, not-yet-teen-
age sensibility was turned up-
side down by fantasies of ecstasy,

betrayal, and despair. I suppose
those pain-ridden hits primed
me for the day, seven or eight
years later, when heartbroken
after a brief affair with a hand-
some, somewhat repressed older
man, I stopped going to the beach
every weekend and my evenly tanned
skin turned white. My parents
no longer insisted I keep my hair
short, so I let it grow long and
unruly. I started chain-smoking.
I tried drugs, but the pills I
stole from medicine cabinets
neither invigorated nor numbed
me, and the joints I hesi-
tantly accepted made me
paranoid. Instead, I drank
wine coolers at a gay bar that
had "Unchained Melody" and
Lesley Gore's version of "Cry
Me A River" on its jukebox,
and went home with anyone who
talked to me. I amused and
terrified friends with tirades
about suicide and unrequited
love, vacillating between deep
depressions and demented gid-
diness. With glee, I invented
whole scenarios of my impending
death—"tragically premature."

*

Earlier this summer,
Michelle and I got
together one night
and split half a gram.
As I precisely divid-
ed our first four
lines, Michelle ex-
citedly named the
anticipated sensations.
The numbness of the
gums was "The Freeze."

The bitter (yet
pleasant) taste
that trickles down
the back of the
throat was "The Drip."
The overall effect
was, in other
words, "A temporary
state of mild
euphoria." Michelle
had just had her
hair frizzed for
the band she was
in and looked
beautiful as she cried
"This be The Freeze!
This be The Drip!"
and wildly danced
around the room.

*

And so, after squandering
the rest of the rent money
on "his" drug, the happy
little thirty-year-old
idiot entertains himself
by staying up until all
hours guzzling Bud after Bud,
smoking endless cigarettes,
and mooning over selected
emotionally evocative favorites
from his eclectic record collec-
tion! How whimsical! And yet:

Love is a growing infection...

Otherwise harmless lyrics
have an ominous aspect
these days, a happening as
impossible to explain as the
changing lines on the palm
of any living hand or the way
the electronic crickets at
the end of this last song

(Eno's "The Great Pretender")
are oddly mingling with
the grating of the real crickets
outside my open window. Soon
many will be faced with the
postcards' gaudy colors in
the souvenir shops up and
down the famous Boulevard—
Hello From Hollywood! and
The Walk Of The Stars! So here
I am: still quite high, al-
beit bankrupt, as always, and
already faced with the first
unwanted indication of sunlight.

III

TO SIR WITH LOVE

My dear fellow artist—
what a surprise it was
to discover that you
have feelings just
like the rest of us.
Life is full of such
interesting twists.
But then you have always
been a source of fascinating
personal disclosure.
I expect nothing less
than complexity from
the man of my dreams.
There's violence in
your work, for instance,
and yet you have the
softest touch. You
have the most attractive
physical assets. And
you certainly know how
to flaunt what you've
got, I'll give you that.
But I would rather you
let me give my heart.

SONNET

The first thirty to sixty days I was

simply insane, if not most mentally

incapable of the simplest tasks: brush

teeth, wash dishes, face, dress for work, drive on

streets, freeways. I had headaches, radio

static, anxiety attacks. Then I

couldn't speak, not in meetings in utter

terror of others and in the fog of

craziest thoughts. The shakes, the coffee pot,

my cigarettes. "Get numbers." "Sit down, shut

up and listen." "Do not drink or use, *no*

matter what." This I did (not alone) and

fell for the most brilliant though mad of them.

But oh I was such a sick one myself.

APRIL INVENTORY

This is typical
autobiographical
stuff: five or
so years ago,
at a bar called
The Doppelganger,
I picked up a guy
who looked a lot
like you. I had
been drinking all
night and was in
a blackout by
the time we got
into bed. I
remember his name
(Harry) and that
the following
morning, before
he left, I handed
him my telephone
number. I was
too intimidated
to ask for his.
He said he'd call
and for a couple
of weeks I waited,
but didn't hear
from him. Of
course the lack
of contact was
proof that I would
never be loved.

Lately, you
are the one I
keep rubbing up
against. I'm such
a sucker for blonds,
especially those
that aren't too
tightly wrapped.
I'm trying not to
resent your openness

—your laughter and
your anger, always
on tap—or your
apparent ease with
possible sex partners.
Last night it almost
worked. I found
a spot close to the
dance floor, stayed
there and looked
for you. The crowd
was mostly Latin,
so you stood out.

I watched how
freely you danced.
You were smiling.
Our eyes met twice.
I wanted to loosen
up, but couldn't
move. I sipped
my mineral water
and smoked cigarette
after cigarette
until I couldn't
stand it anymore.
That old tape
started playing
at full blast,
although this
time I didn't
completely
believe it.

I made a mental
note: "Fear to
be walked through
at a later date,
with somebody
else." Abruptly
I left the bar
and, wondering if
you had noticed,
walked to my car.
I'd parked around

the block, under
a jacaranda.
Its lavender
blossoms blew off
the windshield
as I drove away.

MONDAY, MONDAY

Radio's reality when
the hits just keep
happening: "I want
to kiss like lovers
do..." Why is it
I've always mistaken
these lyrics for my
true feelings? The
disc jockey says it's
spring and instantly
I'm filled with such
joy! Is it possible
that I'm experiencing
nature for the first
time? In the morning
the sun wakes me
and I am genuinely
moved, almost happy
to be alive. For a
couple of weeks it'd
been getting a little
bit brighter every
day. I wasn't aware
of this change until
the morning I noticed
the angle at which
the light hit your
GQ calendar, fully
accentuating the aus-
tere features of this
month's male model, as
I sat in the kitchen,
in your maroon robe,
and waited for my tea
to cool. I was thinking
about my feelings, about
how much I loved the sun
when I was a child and
how I loved the dark
as well, how thrilling
it was to lie in bed
on windy nights and
listen to the sound of

44

bushes and branches being
thrashed about outside.

Actually, that's what
I was thinking while
you were making the tea.
I was staring at the
calendar, at the smoke
from the tip of my
cigarette as it drifted
in the sunlight toward
the open window, when
you set the steaming
fifties-style cup in
front of me. Was it
at this point that
my manner changed?
Your gesture reminded
me of innumerable
mornings spent with
my parents in the pink
kitchen of my childhood.
I remembered my mother,
how she always wore her
gaudy floral bathrobe
and shuffled about in
her bedroom slippers as
she dutifully served us
breakfast. My father
sat alone at one end
of the table, his stern
face all but hidden
behind the front page
of the *Los Angeles Times*.
They seldom spoke. I
felt the tension between
them, watched with sleep-
filled eyes as he gave
her the obligatory kiss
on the cheek, then
clicked his briefcase
shut and, without a word,
walked out the door.

As I was getting dressed,

you grabbed me, kissed
me on the lips, said
something romantic.
I left your apartment
feeling confused, got
on the freeway and
inched my way through
the bumper-to-bumper
traffic. I was confused
about sex, about the
unexpected ambivalence
which, the night before,
prompted my hesitancy
and nonchalant attitude:
"It's late," I said,
"Let's just sleep."
The cars ahead of me
wouldn't budge. I
turned on the radio and
started changing stations.
I was afraid I would
always be that anxious,
that self-obsessed, that
I might never be able
to handle a mature
relationship. Stuck on
the freeway like that,
I was tempted to get
into it, the pain and
the drama, but the mood
soon passed. (After
all, it *is* spring.)
At last, traffic picked
up and I enjoyed the
rest of the drive, kept
the radio on all
the way to work and
listened to all those
songs, though I finally
realized those songs
were no longer my feelings.

MEET THE SUPREMES

When Petula Clark sang "Downtown," I wished I
could go there with her. I wanted to be free
to have fun and fall in love, but from suburbia
the city appeared more distant and dangerous
than it actually was. I withdrew and stayed
in my room, listened to Jackie DeShannon sing
"What The World Needs Now Is Love." I agreed,
but being somewhat morose considered the song
a hopeless plea. I listened to Skeeter Davis'
"The End Of The World" and decided that was
what it would be when I broke up with my first
boyfriend. My head spun as fast as the singles
I saved pennies to buy: "It's My Party," "Give
Him A Great Big Kiss," "(I Want To Be) Bobby's
Girl," "My Guy"—the list goes on. At the age
of ten, I rushed to the record store to get
"Little" Peggy March's smash hit, "I Will Follow
Him." An extreme example of lovesick devotion,
it held down the top spot on the charts for
several weeks in the spring of 1963. "Chapel
Of Love" came out the following year and was
my favorite song for a long time. The girls
who recorded it, The Dixie Cups, originally
called themselves Little Miss & The Muffets.
They cut three hits in quick succession, then
disappeared. I remember almost the exact moment
I heard "Johnny Angel" for the first time: it
came on the car radio while we were driving
down to Laguna Beach to visit some friends of
the family. In the back seat, I set the book I'd
been reading beside me and listened, completely
mesmerized by Shelley Fabares' dreamy, teenage
desire. Her sentimental lyrics continue to move
me (although not as intensely) to this day.
Throughout adolescence, no other song affected
    me quite like that one.
On my transistor, I listened to the Top Twenty
countdown as, week after week, more girl singers
    and groups
came and went than I could keep track of:

                    Darlene Love,
                    Brenda Lee,

Dee Dee Sharp,
Martha Reeves
& The Vandellas,
The Chantels,
The Shirelles,
The Marvelettes,
The Ronettes,
The Girlfriends,
The Rag Dolls,
The Cinderellas,
Alice Wonderland,
Annette, The
Beach-Nuts, Nancy
Sinatra, Little
Eva, Veronica,
The Pandoras,
Bonnie & The
Treasures,
The Murmaids,
Evie Sands,
The Pussycats,
The Patty Cakes,
The Tran-Sisters,
The Pixies Three,
The Toys, The
Juliettes and
The Pirouettes,
The Charmettes,
The Powder Puffs,
Patti Lace &
The Petticoats,
The Rev-Lons,
The Ribbons,
The Fashions,
The Petites,
The Pin-Ups,
Cupcakes,
Chic-Lets,
Jelly Beans,
Cookies, Goodies,
Sherrys, Crystals,
Butterflys,
Bouquets,
Blue-Belles,
Honey Bees,

Dusty Springfield,
The Raindrops,
The Blossoms,
The Petals,
The Angels,
The Halos,
The Hearts,
The Flamettes,
The Goodnight
Kisses, The
Strangeloves,
and The Bitter
Sweets.

I was ecstatic when "He's So Fine" hit the #1 spot.
I couldn't get the lyrics out of my mind and continued
to hum "Doo-lang Doo-lang Doo-lang" long after
puberty ended, a kind of secret anthem. Although
The Chiffons tried to repeat their early success
with numerous singles, none did as well as their
first release. "Sweet Talkin' Guy" came close,
sweeping them back into the Top Ten for a short
time, but after that there were no more hits.
Lulu made her mark in the mid-sixties with "To Sir
    With Love,"
which I would put on in order to daydream about
my junior high algebra instructor. By then I was
a genuine introvert. I'd come home from school,
having been made fun of for carrying my textbooks
like a girl, and listen to song after song from
my ever-expanding record collection. In those
days, no one sounded sadder than The Shangri-Las.
Two pairs of sisters from Queens, they became famous
for their classic "death disc shocker," "Leader Of
    The Pack,"
and for their mod look. They were imitated (but
    never equalled)
by such groups as The Nu-Luvs and The Whyte Boots.
The Shangri-Las stayed on top for a couple of
years, then lost their foothold and split up.
Much later, they appeared in rock 'n' roll revival
shows, an even sadder act since Marge, the fourth
member of the band, had died of an accidental
drug overdose. I started smoking cigarettes around
this time, but wouldn't discover pills, marijuana

or alcohol until my final year of high school.
I loved Lesley Gore because she was always crying
and listened to "As Tears Go By" till the single had
so many scratches I couldn't play it anymore.
I preferred Marianne Faithfull to The Beatles and
The Rolling Stones, was fascinated by the stories
about her heroin addiction and suicide attempt.
She's still around. So is Diana Ross. She made
it to superstardom alone, maintaining the success
she'd previously achieved as the lead singer of
The Supremes, one of the most popular girl groups
of all time. Their debut album was the first LP
I owned. Most of the songs on it were hits—
one would reach the top of the charts as another
hit the bottom. Little did I know, as I listened
to "Nothing But Heartaches" and "Where Did Our Love
Go," that nearly twenty years later I would hit
bottom in an unfurnished Hollywood single, drunk
and stoned and fed up, still spinning those same
old tunes. The friction that already existed
within The Supremes escalated in 1967 as Diana
Ross made plans for her solo career. The impending
split hit Florence the hardest. Rebelliously,
she gained weight and missed several performances,
and was finally told to leave the group. The pain
she experienced in the years that followed was
a far cry from the kind of anguish expressed
in The Supremes' greatest hits. Florence lost
the lawsuit she filed against Motown, failed at
a solo career of her own, went through a bitter
divorce, and ended up on welfare. In this classic
photograph of the group, however, Florence is
smiling. Against a black backdrop, she and Mary
look up at and frame Diana, who stands in profile
and raises her right hand, as if toward the future.
The girls' sequined and tasseled gowns sparkle
as they strike dramatic poses among some Grecian
columns. Thus, The Supremes are captured forever
like this, in an unreal, silvery light. That
moment, they're in heaven. Then, at least for Flo,
begins the long and painful process of letting go.

FOOTNOTE

Nancy's question is
aimed at her mean little heels:
"Are you ready boots?"

ONE FINE DAY

It's a small comfort, at this
point, to know the future is
out of my hands and that there's
a perfect order to everything
that happens. In a somewhat
delusional light, it all makes
sense. For example: the after-
noon you turned me down, I
accidentally chipped the tea
-cup you gave me for Christmas.
I used to cherish your thrift
shop gifts—that terrific '60s
kitsch. Now I'm not sure if
I can forgive myself for being
stuck where I am. There are no
coincidences, and yet the ones
that led me straight to your
door seem like a trail of
bread crumbs some sly devil
left specifically to lead me
astray. No question about it:
I'm lost. We've always lived
in the same cities, on the
same streets, only at different
times. Finally, we find our-
selves at the same address, in
adjacent apartments. Sitting
at my kitchen table, I can't
help but catch snippets of
your conversations. In the
morning, I hear the sound of
your shower; shortly after-
wards, your blender whirs. I
feel like a prisoner or a spy.
Perhaps we'll be lovers in
another life. In this one,
I want to get my feet wet, so
I'll move on. It just makes
me sad to think you might
one day realize you want, as
the song says, the love you
threw away before. Nothing
is certain, of course, but

let me say it in advance,
for my own good: "Good-bye."

IV

MOVIN' WITH NANCY

It is almost time to grow up
I eat my TV dinner and watch
Nancy Sinatra in 1966
All boots and thick blonde hair

I eat my TV dinner and watch
The daughter of Frank Sinatra
All boots and thick blonde hair
She appears on "The Ed Sullivan Show"

The daughter of Frank Sinatra
She sings "These Boots Are Made For Walkin'"
She appears on "The Ed Sullivan Show"
The song becomes a number one hit

She sings "These Boots Are Made For Walkin'"
She sings "Somethin' Stupid" with her father
The song becomes a number one hit
She marries and divorces singer/actor Tommy Sands

She sings "Somethin' Stupid" with her father
She sings "The Last Of The Secret Agents"
She marries and divorces singer/actor Tommy Sands
She sings "How Does That Grab You, Darlin'?"

She sings "The Last Of The Secret Agents"
She sings "Lightning's Girl" and "Friday's Child"
She sings "How Does That Grab You, Darlin'?"
She sings "Love Eyes" and "Sugar Town"

She sings "Lightning's Girl" and "Friday's Child"
She puts herself in the hands of writer/producer Lee Hazelwood
She sings "Love Eyes" and "Sugar Town"
She co-stars with Elvis Presley in *Speedway*

She puts herself in the hands of writer/producer Lee Hazelwood
Three gold records later
She co-stars with Elvis Presley in *Speedway*
She rides on Peter Fonda's motorcycle

Three gold records later
She has developed an identity of her own
She rides on Peter Fonda's motorcycle
The wild angels roar into town

She has developed an identity of her own
Nancy Sinatra in 1966
The wild angels roar into town
It is almost time to grow up

IS YOUR SECRET DATE BEHIND THIS DOOR?

Here is a game full of surprises,
where the players are preparing to
go on a Mystery Date. It may
be a formal dance, a skiing trip,
bowling or a beach party. They must
be "ready" when their date arrives at
the door. The thrill of it is that when
a player opens the door, she has
no idea which date will appear.
She may be ready to go skiing,
only to find, upon opening
the door, the date is dressed in a tux
and holding a corsage box, ready
to escort her to the formal dance!
Worst of all, she may open the door
to find the "Dud," who is shabbily
clad, and lose her valuable time
getting rid of him. She must throw the
die and advance her playing piece clock-
wise around the board. The first girl to
open the door and find the date for
which she is appropriately dressed
is the lucky one, and wins the game.

TWIGGY

Model a mod outfit.
Pose for pictures at
the airport. Wave
hello to teen fans.

FLOWER POWER

for Jim Isermann

Red and
blue mod
poppy.

Orange
and green
optical
jonquil.

Pink
paisley
daisy.

Yellow
psyche-
delic
daffodil.

DOUBLE TROUBLE

Patty:

"Hi, Mom! I'm home!"
I shouted as I burst
through the front door.
"Hello, dear." I dashed
upstairs, threw my books
on the floor, tossed
on a stack of singles
and flopped down on
the bed. Chad & Jeremy
sent me instantly to
Dreamsville. I rolled
over and reached for
my princess phone. "Hi,
Sue Ellen." "HI! Oh,
Patty!" she gushed,
"You're absolutely the
talk of the campus! I
mean you're practically
a celebrity!" We gig-
gled about how I'd
been dragged to the
principal's office
for cutting my geome-
try class and spying
on Richard in the
boys' locker room.
"Have you told your
dad yet?" "And miss
my date with Richard
tonight? Not on your
life! I'm meeting him
at the Shake Shop at
eight." There was a
knock on my door. "I
gotta run, Sue Ellen.
See you tomorrow." We
hung up. "Come in!"
It was Dad. I'd never
seen him look so mad.
"I received a call
from the principal

Cathy:

From the beginning, I
was opposed to Patty's
"wild" idea. It just
didn't seem feasible.
Her enthusiasm, how-
ever, was dizzying.
After listening to her
plan, she persuaded
me to exchange clothes
with her. Frantically,
she threw on my white
blouse, plaid skirt,
knee socks and oxfords
while, reluctantly, I
slipped into her sweat
shirt, blue jeans and
scruffy tennis shoes.
Next, she brushed her
flip into a pageboy
and wiped the makeup
off her face, then
spun around, brushed
my pageboy into a flip
and applied her fa-
vorite Yardley shade
(Liverpool Pink) to my
pursed lips. We stood
back and looked at each
other in the mirror. It
was perfectly uncanny:
I couldn't even tell us
apart. Patty squealed
with delight and grabbed
my hands. "Now, Cath,"
she coached, "Try not
to act so brainy, or
we'll never pull this
off!" She picked up a
few library books and
said "Bye-eee," then
glided out the door. I

of your school today," he said. My heart just about stopped. "Gosh, Pop-O..." "Don't 'Gosh, Pop-O' me, young lady. *You* are grounded. For the next two weeks, you're to stay home and study every night. You're to be in bed by nine o'clock. No phone privileges." "OH!" I cried. "No music." He switched off the phonograph. "And clean up this mess!" The door slammed behind him. I moaned and buried my head in the pillow. My whole life was ruined! What about my date??? How in the world could I be in two places at once? Just then, Cathy came into the room. "Hello, Patty," she smiled. I stared at her. She blinked back. "Anything wrong?" "Yes! No! I mean LIKE WOW!" I yelled as I jumped up and down. "I have the *wildest* idea!!!"

sat down and studied for my geometry midterm. At one point, Ross stuck his head in the room. "What's up, Sis?" he asked. I took a deep breath, turned around and said "Scram, brat!" in the harshest tone of voice I could muster. He made a nasty face and stomped off. The real test came at nine o'clock, when Uncle Martin stopped by to turn out the lights. "I hope you understand this is for your own good," he said. "I dig, Pop-O," I uttered with a weak smile. He didn't seem the least bit suspicious, so I slid into Patty's bed and blew a goodnight kiss at him. Then, for a convincing finishing touch, I blew another kiss across the room, at Patty's heart-shaped framed photograph of Frankie Avalon.

THE MUNSTERS

Among cobwebs and
dust, Lily sits in
the parlor reading
this month's issue
of *Tomb and Garden*.
In the lab, Grandpa
hangs upside down,
dreaming of fara-
way Transylvania.
Up in his bedroom,
Eddie sleeps off
the effects of last
night's full moon.
When the doorbell
rings (to the tune
of a funeral march),
Spot roars flames.
Herman stomps to
the front door and
opens it. Hair on
end, Marilyn's date
runs screaming down
Mockingbird Lane.

RERUNS

Splash!

Like a rock, Elly
May's cake sank to the bottom
of the "ceement" pond.

*

In Outer Space

Judy Jetson spins
a disc and does the Orbit
to "Comet Of Love."

*

With a Little Grin

Morticia snipped off
the rose and placed the stem in
the tombstone-shaped vase.

*

Patty to Cathy

"While you study as
me, I'll leave as you, then go
as me on my date!"

*

Housework

Samantha looked at
the dirty dishes. "Just this
once," she thought, and twitched.

*

New Year's Eve

The cork popped off the
bottle and, effervescent,
Jeannie overflowed.

*

Honey in the Flesh

She knew how to use
her high-voltage curves like an
unconcealed weapon.

*

Batman and Robin

hang by threads above
a bubbling vat of acid.
To be continued...

*

Model Children

Kitten told the truth.
Princess set aside her pride.
Bud made right his wrong.

*

Island Girls

Mary Ann dons one
of Ginger's dresses, but it
falls flat on her chest.

*

Gossip

Gidget and Larue
knock heads as they press their ears
to the princess phone.

*

Fred's Breakfast

With a club, Wilma
cracked open the three-minute
pterodactyl egg.

*

Puberty

Wally pounds on the
bathroom door. "C'mon Beav! You've
been in there for hours!"

       *

Fractured Fairy Tale

This kissing princess
was such a dog that the frog
she smacked simply croaked.

       *

Green Acres

The smoke from Lisa's
burnt pancakes slowly blackens
the fresh country air.

       *

The Mod Squad

Julie, Pete and Linc
bust some thugs, then head back to
their pad to turn on.

       *

Like Bird or Balloon

Sister Bertrille fades
to a speck in the blue sky
above San Tanco.

V

NOVEMBER

for Christopher Harrity

11/4

Sunlight
(the drapes
only par-
tially drawn)
on orange
carpet. Wall
lamp (pink,
green and
black) by
Isermann.
Stereo (on
floor). Stack
of records:
The Go•Go's,
Laurie An-
derson, Lin-
da Ronstadt.
In black
wire rack:
this month's
Vanity Fair,
VALLEY OF
THE DOLLS,
*Barbie: The
Magazine
For Girls,*
et cetera.
Faded green
cushions on
black chair.
Black lamp
(thanks to
Christopher)
on small round
table. Pink
futon. Star-
burst clock
(red, yellow,
blue), also

by Isermann.
On an end
table (blond
wood): two
spiritual
books, candle,
ashtray and
(thanks to Joe,
Christopher's
beau) red car-
nations in
a white art
nouveau vase.

11/9

Morning fog.
I can't think
clearly yet.

*

Two cups of tea
(Earl Grey in-
stead of Lipton
for a change)
and lots of
cigarettes later.
Not much better.
Suppose these
last addictions
are beginning
to fail me?
Then what?

Oh, maybe just
one more cup.

*

The doorbell
(waiting for
the water
to boil).
Flowers!
Sign here.
What a de-
lightful
surprise!
From Bob R.
A dozen
red roses
swathed in
baby's breath.
I leave a
"thank you
so much"
message on
his phone

machine.

*

Those amazing
girl groups
strike again:
"Da Doo Ron
Ron." "I
Have A Boy-
friend" is
a wonderful
but obscure
number by
The Chiffons.
A truly upbeat
little ditty.

*

Only one piece
of mail today.
I tear open
the envelope.
Some sort of
announcement of—
Pat's death.
It takes my
breath away.
A heart attack,
the note from
her husband
says. I have
to sit down.
Poor Pat.
Patricia Capps,
Rachel's mother.
I wait, but
no tears come.
Rachel's been
gone how long
now? Over six
years. I call
Kathy. She's
out, so I tell

her daughter
the news. I
light a candle
and another
cigarette, then
turn over
the tape.

＊

"Wait!
Oh yes,
wait a minute
Mr. Postman..."

Christopher knocks
on my window, then
the door. "Come
in." "There was an
awful accident on
the freeway! I was
stuck for over two
hours! I'm *so* mad!"
He goes home to
sleep. I sit down
to write. A little
later, Christopher
calls. He likes
the new message on
my phone machine: me
followed by about
thirty seconds of
"Blame It On The
Bossa Nova." "What
are you up to?" he
asks. "Writing."
"Oh, how's it going?"
"Not well," I tell
him. "All I've
come up with is:
A cold and quiet
November night."

11/21

A cold and quiet
November night.
I sit on the floor
next to the heater.
In front of me:
old Smith-Corona,
green loose-leaf
notebook, cigarettes,
lighter and ash-
tray (the one that
Christopher bought
at a thrift shop
in San Francisco:
shaped like a comma,
yellow with orange
specks), diction-
ary, teacup, pen.
The flowers (bur-
gundy mums) that
Joe brought last
week are beginning
to wilt. New ones
would be nice. No
music, not tonight.
It's quiet. A cold
(although quite
cozy here by the
heater) and quiet
November night.

Friday evening,
Christopher,
Joe and I lis-
ten to *Televi-
sion's Greatest
Hits* (themes
from "Green
Acres," "The
Addams Family,"
"The Patty
Duke Show,"
and so forth)
as we primp
in front of
the full-length
mirror in
Christopher's
bedroom. Joe
wears a tan-
gerine cardigan
and orange and
turquoise Ban-
Lon pullover.
Christopher
wears his new
over-dyed pur-
ple Perry Ellis
sweater. Except
for a brown and
tan plaid muf-
fler and white
high-tops, I
wear all black.
Jay arrives and
we're off to the
1985 Queen of the
Universe contest
(for female im-
personators) at
"the meteoric
Mayflower Ball-
room." Our table
is in front, right

below the stage.
We order cokes.
The lights go
down. The show
opens with an act
featuring Empress
LeRey as a giant
spider with eight
huge furry arms.
On either side
of her, suspended
in webs, several
half-naked boys
writhe and con-
tort their faces
in fear. After
a few more num-
bers, the stage
is cleared. Then,
one by one, the
contestants ap-
pear and parade
on the runway.
Christopher and
Jay roll their
eyes. Joe whis-
tles and shouts:
"¡Ay Chica!" I
look up, applaud
and laugh. Such
exotic outfits!
Many feathers,
veils, jewelled
hairpieces and
heels. Miss Phil-
ippines, Miss Viet
Nam, Miss Hawaii,
Miss Saudi Arabia.
Miss Egypt is
carried onstage
by four men in
loincloths and
chains. The aged
Miss Iceland is
dressed as an

enormous silver
and white snow-
flake. The judges
confer and Miss
Iceland is an-
nounced the winner
of the costume
competition. As
she rushes out to
accept the trophy,
part of her snow-
flake-shaped head-
dress catches on
a lighting grid
and sparks fly.
"I'd love to see
what she does for
the 4th of July,"
someone says.
The swimsuit
competition is
next, but we get
up to leave during
the fifteen min-
ute intermission.

Saturday morning,
John and Louise
(my mother's aunt)
and I drive four
hours up the coast
to see my parents,
who've recently re-
tired. The time
passes fast, with-
out much small talk.
Light traffic. We
stop in Santa Bar-
bara: Louise buys
us lunch at a res-
taurant on State
St. and complains
about the slow
service. Back
on the road, she
worries about the
rain ("It's only
sprinkling, Aunt
Louise.") and
that we'll miss
our exit, which is
next to impossible:
there's just one
for the entire city
of Nipomo. West
on Tefft (a coun-
try road) to Rose,
left to Chandra,
right to La Loma
(which Chandra
turns into). My
parents' new home
is beautiful: a
pale yellow and
brick ranch house
on a large (over
an acre) lot. No
lawn yet. They're
at the front door:

Mom and Dad, Lin-
da (my sister, re-
cently separated)
and her two kids,
Kristy and Ryan.
We all smile, kiss,
hug and shake hands.
Rita (the Doberman)
sniffs and follows
us. Skipper (the
rat terrier) yaps
and wags in his
little cage (he'll
pee on the furni-
ture if loose).
We sit in the
family room and
visit. Ryan looks
up at me and asks,
"Who are you?"
"He's very bright
for his age," my
mother says. My
father goes out-
side to get more
firewood. Linda
sets the table.
My mother puts
dinner together.
It starts raining
harder and harder
as it gets dark.

11/24

Last night, after
Kristy performed
her baton routine,
we sat in the liv-
ing room and played
several games of
Old Maid. She lost
each time, but didn't
seem to mind. Then
we played with Lin-
da's ancient Chatty
Cathy. I was amazed
it still worked. We
slid the miniature
records in and out
of the doll's side
and pulled the ring
at the back of her
neck. "I always eat
my vegetables," she
said. "Everybody
likes good girls."
Ryan brought out
and demonstrated
his Glow Turtle:
press his stomach
and his face lights
up! We laughed and
played with toys
until their bedtime.
Still excited, they
couldn't sleep.
John stayed up and
talked with my mother.
I laid down on the
couch and was out
like a light.

At the breakfast
table, Aunt Louise
says: "Is David

always this grumpy
in the morning?"
She doesn't real-
ize I can hear her.
"Bitch, bitch, bitch,"
I whisper to my
mother in the kitchen.

*

Linda and the children
put on raincoats and go
to church. My father
watches football on TV.
Aunt Louise works on a
crossword. She's staying
through Thanksgiving.
My mother warms up the
car, takes John and me
on a little tour of the
area. A golf course and
half-completed condomin-
ium tract, some other
houses they had looked
at. "Yours is better,"
I tell her. Beautiful
downtown Nipomo: the
post office and a li-
quor store. Santa Maria.
Pismo Beach. The local
nuclear research plant.

*

We say good-bye in
the rain. I try not
to get Christopher's
suede jacket wet. My
mother pulls me a-
side and says: "I
worry about you.
Look at Rock Hudson
—with all his money.
Be careful." I tell
her not to worry a-

bout me, kiss her
on the cheek. We
wave and drive off.
It rains all the way
back to Los Angeles.

11/27

My caseload
at the Housing
Authority is
always crazy
the day before
a holiday week-
end. I'm glad
when it's time
to go. Traffic's
slow on the Gold-
en State; no ac-
cidents, though.
I call Christopher
the minute I get
home. "Come over,"
he says. I bring
some tea bags
and we tell each
other about our
days. Then we
run out to the
video store and
rent a few movies
for tomorrow:
Little Women,
The Thin Man
and (my idea)
The Parent Trap.
Christopher calls
me a "big Teen
Queen" and we
both crack up.
Home again, I
listen to the
messages on my
phone machine.
Jay says he has
to cancel his
Friday night
get-together
due to "tech-
nical diffi-
culties" with

his visiting
mother. Kathy
says she's al-
ways blamed it
on the Bossa
Nova. "Call
me." Amy says:
"Happy Thanks-
giving (almost)."

I've only been awake
a little while when
Christopher calls.
"Joe's in the shower,"
he says, "I told him
you and I already made
plans to pick up my
mother. Will you go?"
"Sure." I pull on a
sweater, brush my teeth
and dash next door.
"In here!" he calls,
"I just put the bird
in the oven." I smoke
a cigarette while he
cleans up. "Could you
hand me that vase?"
"Sure." A Bauer. He
puts fresh flowers in it.
"What would you do with-
out a boyfriend who
works for a florist?"
I ask. "I don't know.
There! Let's go."
Joe sticks his wet
head out of the bath-
room. "Good-bye, girls."
"I'm mad about you!"
Christopher yells as
we hurry out the door,
"Don't forget the yams."

*

At the airport, we look
at the magazines and
trinkets in the gift
shop, then sit and talk
until Jody's flight
arrives. We greet her
at Gate 5. Christopher
gives her a big hug.
"Hello, you." Jody

wears a trench coat,
hat and boots. "It
was raining when we
left Oakland," she says.
"We've had some here,"
I tell her, "but it's
clear today." We follow
the arrows to the bag-
gage claim area and
wait for her suitcases
to appear on the con-
veyor. "I'm so glad you
could come," Christopher
says, "We're going to
have a *fabulous* time!"

*

I open all the windows
in the apartment. I
fold the sheets, blan-
kets and futon. I dust
and vacuum, get the
laundry going, wash
the dishes, throw the
dead mums in the trash.
I sit down and drink
a cup of tea, call
Bob and Sheree. "Happy
Thanksgiving!" I say
to their answering
machine. I call Kathy.
"Happy Thanksgiving!"
She says she got a
note from Pat's husband,
thanking us for the
flowers. "Can you
stop by later?" I
tell her I probably
won't be able to.
I call my mother.
"Happy Thanksgiving!"
She says my father is
taking her and Louise
out to dinner tonight.

"Someone wants to say
hello to you." "Hi,
Uncle Dave?" "Hi, Ryan.
Happy Thanksgiving!"

*

Christopher leaves a
message while I'm in
the shower: "Dinner's
almost ready, darling.
Where are you?" I
dress up and go over.
They're all in the
kitchen. "It smells
like Thanksgiving,"
I say. Christopher
hands me a glass of
Perrier in a long-
stemmed wine glass
and a shrimp cocktail
in a tumbler with a
copper holder. He
also hands me his
Polaroid. I take a
few pictures: Jody
lifting a pot off the
stove, Joe grinning in
front of the refriger-
ator, Christopher
carving the turkey.
The food's beautiful-
ly arranged on an
orange and green
'40s drapery panel
spread across a blond
Chinese Moderne desk:
homemade cranberry
sauce in a Roseville
dish, stuffing (with
nuts) in an apricot
Vernonware bowl,
broccoli, wild rice,
warm whole wheat rolls.
Joe puts his yams

(Von's canned) in
a fluted orange bowl.
"They have honey and
brown sugar on them,"
he says. Christopher
sets down a platterful
of light and dark meat.
"Come and get it!"
We serve ourselves
on square Franciscan
plates, sit in the
bedroom and watch
The Thin Man on the
VCR. Christopher:
"Myrna Loy is beau-
tiful." Jody: "Oh,
yes." Joe: "Look at
that dress!" Me:
"Dolly Tree outdid
herself." I eat fast,
get up and fix some
tea, slice a large
piece of pumpkin
pie. The three of
them are crowded to-
gether on the bed.
I sit on the floor.
"What's wrong?" Joe
asks me towards the
end of the movie.
"Nothing." "You're so
quiet. What's wrong?"
"*Nothing*." When he
asks again, I snap
at him: "Stop it,
please." Everyone
looks at me. I take
my dishes into the
kitchen, set them in
the sink. I wait a
few minutes, then go
back into the bedroom.
"I'm going to take
off. Everything was
delicious. Thank you."

Christopher jumps up,
walks me to the front
door. "Are you alright?"
he asks. "I'm fine,"
I say. "Do you want
to take any food home
with you?" "No, I'm
stuffed. Thank you,
though. Goodnight."

11/29

After a late break-
fast, we drive around
to some bookstores
so Christopher can
deliver samples of
the 1986 She-Male
"Pin-Up" Calendar
("Transsexual super-
stars in the most
intimate settings"),
which he designed for
Kim Christy Productions.
At A Different Light,
I run into Larry.
"What are you doing
tonight?" he asks.
"I don't have any
plans." "Why don't
you stop by my place.
I'm having some people
over." "I'll try to
make it. Thanks."
On the way to West
Hollywood, we stop
and look through Have
A Nice Day, a new shop
on Melrose full of
'60s stuff: lava lamps,
a red beanbag chair,
clear plastic pillows,
daisy pins, Peter Max
ashtrays and scarves,
a troll doll with wild
orange hair, Happy Face
place mats, television
sets that resemble space
helmets. We take turns
sitting in a magenta-
lined egg-shaped iso-
lation chair. More
bookstores: Drake's,
Unicorn, Dorothy's Sur-
render. We end up at

George Sand. Christopher
hands the calendar to
the woman behind the
counter. "Would you
give this to the person
who does your purchasing?"
he asks, "A cover letter's
included." The woman
opens the wrapper and
looks at a few of the
pictures. "I don't
think we'd be interested
in presenting women in
such a sexist fashion,"
she says as she passes
it back to him, "Perhaps
you should try some of
those adult bookstores
in Hollywood." "They're
not women," Christopher
tells her, "They're men."
"Really," the woman says,
"That is even worse."

*

Before Christopher re-
turns the tapes, I put
a new outgoing message
on my phone machine: a
song from *The Parent Trap*,
Hayley Mills (as iden-
tical twins) singing
"Let's Get Together"
("Yeah, yeah, yeah").

*

Christopher takes a nap
on the black-and-white
striped chaise in the
living room. Janet (his
cat) curls up in Jody's
lap and sleeps while
Jody and I watch two ep-

isodes of the *Twilight
Zone* marathon. In the
first, a mute Agnes
Moorehead is terrorized
by two tiny, toylike
spacemen. Grunting and
groaning, she captures
one in a burlap sack
and throws him in the
fireplace, then squashes
the other as he tries
to escape in the little
spaceship. Her ordeal
is over. But there's
a twist: the intruders
were actually astronauts
from earth, whereas Agnes
was a giant on a distant
planet. In the second
episode, Anne Francis (as
a lustful country girl)
sells her soul to a witch
in order to win the heart
of the man she loves.
The spell works: he wants
to marry her. She must,
however, pay the devil
his due: every night at
midnight, she is trans-
formed into a ferocious
leopard. This is not ex-
actly what she had in mind.
At the end, she's cornered
by the townsmen and shot.

＊

Driving down Vermont,
I see the first sign
of Christmas: a lit tree
in a second-story win-
dow. By the time I get
to Larry's, the party's
in full swing: at least
thirty men crammed in-

to his small apartment.
I stand in the kitchen,
smoke and drink a couple
of Diet Cokes. I talk
to two guys—John and
Kurt—and am attracted
to both of them. "Nice
talking with you," John
says when he leaves,
"Hope I see you around."
"Same here," I say.
After the party breaks
up, Kurt and I go to
Astro's, "the coffee
shop of the future."
We order hamburgers.
He's twenty-one, from
Sacramento, works at
a record store on Sunset.
Walking out to the park-
ing lot, I ask him if
he wants to spend the
night with me. "I'd like
that," he says. And then:
"I only have safe sex."
"Same here," I say.

I wake up in the middle of
the night and can't get back
to sleep. Carefully, I lift
Kurt's arm and slide out of
bed. I go to the bathroom,
then sit in the kitchen and
smoke until it begins to get
light outside. I take a
shower, shave, straighten
a few things, put some water
on. When Kurt wakes, I make
him a cup of tea. "I had
trouble sleeping," I tell
him. "I didn't," he says,
"This thing is comfortable."
He pats the futon. I light
a cigarette with one that's
almost out. Kurt says he
just stopped smoking a couple
of weeks ago. I tell him
I quit for over two months
earlier this year and that
I plan to try again soon.
Kurt gets dressed and I
drive him to his car, which
is parked across the street
from Larry's building. We
sit for a moment. "Thank
you for last night." "Sure."
Kurt smiles and hops out
of the car. I reach over
and lock the door. I pull
away, turn right at the
light, and drive up Vermont
towards the post office.

It starts to rain again in
the afternoon. I wake up
from a nap, turn on the heat
and sit down at my desk to
type for a while. Through

the wall, I hear Christopher
and his mother laugh and talk.
I call and say: "You sound
like a roomful of people."
"We are!" Christopher ex-
claims. He invites me out
to eat with them. I hesitate.
"I'll loan you an overcoat,"
he says. "Okay." We drive
across town in the rain.
Later, if it lets up, we'll
window-shop in Hollywood or
Beverly Hills. Christopher
pulls into the French Quarter,
but the lot's full. We opt
for Noura, a Greek restau-
rant just east of La Cienega.
We park, make a run for it
and shake ourselves off in-
side the door. We're seated
at a corner table. The wait-
er brings menus and a basket
of pita bread. Christopher
and Jody order the Mediter-
ranean salad. I can't decide,
so I try the Taster's Delight:
eggplant, tabbouleh, stuffed
grapeleaves. After we eat,
I get up to look at the bak-
lava and notice a jar of
madeleines next to the cash
register. "Here's dessert,"
I say as I set a small plate
on the table. "One apiece.
Compliments of Marcel Proust."
"That's right," says Jody,
Remembrance of Things Past."
I take the first bite. "I
tried to read him in college,"
I say, "but only made it
through half of *Swann's Way.*
It was Rachel's copy. In
fact, I still had it when
she died." I tell them about
the accident: July 5, 1979,

2 a.m., the drunk driver who
passed out and hit us head-on.
"He and Rachel were killed
instantly. She was driving.
Christian, her boyfriend,
was in the front seat. I
was in the back. We were
both injured. I was in the
hospital for a long time."
I push the plate towards
Christopher. He eats the
second madeleine, then tells
us that he inherited a com-
plete set of Proust after
his ex-lover's mysterious
death in 1976. "John read
a lot," he says. "His books
are packed away somewhere.
You know, at Land's End in
San Francisco, there's ac-
tually a sign that says:
'Be careful while climbing
rocks: You may be swept to
your death.' The city must
have put it there." The wait-
er comes by with our check.
Jody picks up the last little
shell-shaped cake and exam-
ines it. "Nance and Mother
and I used to bake these,"
she says. "Oddly enough, I
sent Nance a madeleine tin
for Christmas last year."
She pauses to take a bite.
"When Mother died, I told
our friends the service was
going to be as simple as pos-
sible. Instead of sending
flowers, I suggested they
plant something in their yards.
The idea just popped into my
head. Nance planted a blue
rose in Colorado Springs.
There's also a daphne bush in
Ferndale, a blossoming cactus

in Tucson, and another rose, one with the loveliest cream-colored petals, which a dear friend planted in memory of her in Moraga, California."

VI

LIVING DOLL

for Sheree Levin

The night we met, I was wearing one of my most exquisite ensembles: formal, floor-length gown with flowing train (in the elegance of pink satin), pearl necklace and drop earrings, pink dancing pumps with silver glitter, white elbow gloves and fur stole. An enchanted evening! I can still hear those distant harps and violins, can still recall how the laughter and chatter of the other guests magically dissolved as we sipped champagne on the lush, moonlit terrace. "He's such a doll!" I thought. "This must be love at first sight!" Right then, I decided I wanted to spend the rest of my days gazing into that dreamboat's blue eyes.

The following Sunday, Ken picked me up for a drive in the country. I took the high fashion road with my beige sweater and striped pants, a car coat fastened with toggles, a straw hat that ties with a red scarf, and wedgies to match...perfect for a lunch-stop in a picturesque village. Before I slid into the passenger seat, I noticed the license plate on Ken's sports car. It said MATTEL. I later learned he was the youngest and fastest-rising executive the company had ever employed.

At that point, I was a little bewildered about the direction of my own future. My modeling career seemed to be going nowhere. The photo sessions, fan mail, and fashion shows that had once brought me fame were tapering off. I simply wasn't up for it anymore. (It isn't easy being a teen-age model at twenty-five!) Besides, I wanted to do something different. Oh, I had tried just about everything. As a ballerina, I danced before kings and queens as the Sugar Plum Fairy, costumed in a shimmering silver tutu. As a stewardess, I took off for sky adventures in a navy blue uniform with flight insignia on cap and jacket. I'd even been a registered nurse and cured patients in my trim white uniform and silk-lined cape. Before I met Ken, I had been toying with the idea of pursuing a singing career. Although I'd started to appear at some of the nightclubs around town, I could tell this endeavor would never really get off the ground. The feelings I found myself developing for Ken gave my life new meaning, a definite direction. He seemed to fix it for me.

The next couple of months, we were practically inseparable. We went sailing and ice-skating. We played tennis at an exclusive country club. On our alpine holiday, I sported a swaggering leather coat, a striped t-shirt with jaunty hood, and knit mittens. Often, after cocktails, I twirled on dance floors in a feminine flower print accented with a fancy sash or a powder blue corduroy jumper with colorful felt appliques and bouffant petticoat. For a garden party, I cultivated a cotton candy look: rosebuds, ruffles, and dainty pink bow at waist. I blossomed out for a fund-raising banquet in a buttercup yellow sheath frosted with sheer overskirt, smart hat, and a bouquet of spring posies to complete the pretty picture. But did Ken notice? Was it my imagination, or was he growing more and more remote?

I sensed something was amiss the night I debuted my new act at The Pink Lady Lounge. Didn't Ken realize what an important event it was? There were no tasteful floral arrangements, no expensive chocolates or vintage wines. I'd spent hours at the dressing room vanity in a frenzy of false eyelashes, mascara, powder puffs, lipsticks, and bobby pins. And still I didn't look right! I was completely beside myself. I'd misplaced one of my gold hoop earrings. I couldn't get the ribbon tied around my ponytail. I could barely fasten my bead necklace. At the last minute, I managed to slip into my dramatic black glitter-gown, the one with bare shoulders and a rose corsage on its netted flounce. I pulled on my long black gloves just as a stagehand ushered me into the wings...and before I knew it, I was standing at the microphone, in the middle of my first number, pink scarf in hand. Beyond the glare of the spotlight, I recognized a couple at one of the front tables. It was Allen and Midge. But where was Ken? I nearly collapsed several times during my performance. Afterwards, I kept the bartender company until last call, then took a taxi home.

What went wrong? Why won't he answer my messages? Whenever I phone his office, the curt receptionist says he's either in a conference or at the gym. Why won't he let me get close to him? Lately, all I do is mope around my apartment in a yellow terrycloth robe (with a big monogrammed "B" on the breast pocket). I oversleep and keep the drapes drawn all day. I'm gaining weight. There are dark circles under my eyes. I should try to pull myself together, but what about the plans we made? What about my Dream House and its complete suite of modern, slim-line furniture? What about my magnificent church wedding dress? It's fit for a princess: formal train, diamond tiara, tiered bridal veil, and billowing layers of flowered nylon tulle. What about my trousseau...my embroidered peignoir or my full-length pink negligee with its Grecian bodice and low-cut back? Are my dreams as flimsy? Are they as transparent as that?

A MILLION TO ONE

When we were little kids, I used to tease him about the way money always appeared in his path. I'd say: "You attract money like a magnet attracts metal." It was true. One time, when a woman strolling ahead of us dropped her pocketbook on the sidewalk, some change popped out and started rolling towards him. "How do you like that?!" he exclaimed. I just about fainted. Those shiny silver coins rolled *uphill* and landed right at Richie's feet!

As the years passed, Richie refined his technique. By setting aside half of his generous allowance every week, he accumulated stacks and stacks of cash, which he stuffed into a giant safe. Following his father's advice, he invested his savings in Rich Enterprises. Stocks and bonds, oil fields, gold and diamond mines...his assets skyrocketed overnight. He was the only millionaire to ever enroll at Richville High, and was treated better than any dignitary or movie star. A red carpet would unfold as his sports car pulled up at school each morning. Between classes, girls flocked around him for autographs. The principal even allowed a special telephone to be installed in his homeroom desk. In our senior year, when he ran against Reginald for class president, posters of Richie's adorable blond head were plastered all over campus. Naturally, Richie won the election by a landslide. Afterwards, Reggie threw a big fit. He turned bright green and claimed that his lifelong rival had unfairly gained votes by erecting a free amusement park on the Rich estate during the campaign. Of course no one paid attention to him. Nothing could tarnish Richie's perfect image. About this time, however, things began to get out of hand.

It all started one afternoon while we were studying together in his private library. Without warning, Richie leapt across the table and tried to kiss me—on the lips! I managed to fend him off, pretending I was too worried about my algebra midterm to think of anything else. Imagine my shock when I walked in to take the exam and discovered an entire classroom filled with long-stemmed red roses and, draped above the blackboard, a gigantic banner that said: GOOD LUCK, GLORIA!!! My instructor and fellow students were impressed, but I was so embarrassed I couldn't concentrate and flunked the test.

Shortly after that, Richie took up skywriting and, out of the blue, composed a whole love letter for me (and everyone else!) to read. He showered me with expensive gifts, surprised me with extravagant picnics, whisked me off on spur-of-the-moment shopping sprees and exotic trips. I tried to avoid him, but it was impossible. Compulsively, he monitored my every move. If I so much as sneezed, a complete hospital staff would show up at my front door. There were armored trucks, round-the-clock security guards, booby traps, alarms, and the craziest kinds of devices, including a blimp camouflaged as a cloud that transported me to and from school. When I objected to all of this, Richie was adamant. "You're too easy a target," he insisted. "Look what happened to Freckles and Peewee." I thought about the ghastly kidnapping of Richie's best friends and decided that he was right. Since he had appeared on the cover of *Fortune*, the cover of *Money*, and the cover of *Success*, every criminal on the globe was out to get Richie's riches.

Then came the night of the Senior Prom, which was to be held in the Prom Room at the Rich mansion. Surrounded by a squad of police escorts, Cadbury arrived in a solid-gold limousine to drive me to the dance. The festivities could be seen in the distance: spotlights, helicopters, huge white and silver balloons. The house itself was lit like an immense birthday cake. As we passed through the gilded R-shaped gates, the most breathtaking display of fireworks erupted above the estate. That's when it hit me. Instinctively, I knew something disastrous was about to happen. Before I could order Cadbury to turn back, Richie jumped in beside me, tied a blindfold around my eyes, and pulled me from the car. Ignoring my protests, he directed me up the stairs, into the mansion, and through an endless maze of corridors in the west wing. It seemed like we walked for miles. When we finally stopped, Richie lifted my hand and slipped something heavy on one of my fingers. Then he removed the blindfold. And there we stood—right in the middle of the dance floor!

Instantly, flashbulbs popped all around us. I squinted at a mob of reporters and cameramen. Beyond them, in bleachers, hundreds of teenagers applauded and cheered. I felt light-headed, unsteady. Confetti and streamers landed on everyone as a band started singing, "Here comes the bride..." Richie's parents squeezed through the crowd, babbling congratulations. I glanced at Mrs. Rich's dazzling jewels, at Mr. Rich's glistening emerald tiepin, at Richie's sparkling baby-blue eyes. I looked up as he raised my hand for photographs: on my finger, the largest diamond I'd ever seen glittered and flashed. I gasped and pulled back. Everything began to blur together: the flickering lights, the smiling faces, the brilliant white engagement ring...

As if a trap door slid open underneath me, I dropped into a pitch-black bottomless pit. I fell until my formal puffed around my neck like a parachute, then weightlessly floated downwards. All of a sudden, an enormous newspaper came spinning out of the darkness. It was the front page of *The Richville Gazette.* I read the headline as it whirled past: POOR LITTLE RICH BOY WEDS CHILDHOOD SWEETHEART. Another newspaper spun towards me: TEEN MILLIONAIRE AND REDHEAD TIE KNOT. Impishly, Richie winked, grinned, and snickered as he sailed by on the covers of *People, Life, Newsweek,* and *Time.* He materialized on immense Monopoly money, comic books, a playing card (The King of Diamonds), a row of soup cans, an Indian-head penny, and a postage stamp. A giant desk calendar drifted above me, shedding the days of the year like dead leaves. This was followed by a procession of oversized timepieces: a sundial, an hourglass, a stopwatch, and a heart-shaped windup alarm clock that ticktocked so fast it burst into a mass of gears and springs. Outlined in blinking neon, a mammoth slot machine appeared and registered three, four, five double R's, which triggered an endless waterfall of shimmering silver coins. Several yachts emerged, then an ocean liner, a Rolls-Royce, a train, an airplane and, through a hoop of fire, speedboats pulling women in gold lamé bathing suits on water skis. A race car (with Richie in it) zoomed by and emitted a thick cloud of exhaust, making me cough and choke. Out of the smoke flew a roulette wheel, a silver tea service, a cash register, a tennis court, a treasure chest, a Christmas tree dripping with rubies and diamond icicles, a bubble gum machine filled with multicolored gems, a litter of dalmatians with cent symbols instead of spots, and a swimming pool shaped like a gigantic dollar sign. A chorus line of oysters pranced out and circled the pool. In unison, they opened their shells to exhibit an exquisite string of gleaming pearls, then slammed shut and jumped into the deep end, splashing water all over me. A colossal bottle of French champagne spun around, stopped, popped off its cork, and doused me with the force of a fire hose. Rumbling like thunder, a gusher shot straight up, splattering me with black oil. When it subsided, I found myself face-to-face with a full-length portrait of Richie in his old age. He looked exactly the same, only taller! The painting swung forward, unleashing an avalanche of cash from the wall safe hidden behind it. Like feathers to tar, dollar bills stuck to my hair and dress. Next, a storm cloud settled overhead and pelted me with pennies, nickels, dimes, quarters, half dollars, silver dollars, shillings, francs, pesos, yen, bread, lettuce, moola, loot, and smackeroos. After the downpour, a heavenly yellow halo glowed above the pot of gold at the end of a rainbow. Meanwhile, below me, a money sack began to suck everything up like a huge vacuum cleaner. As the newspapers, the slot machine, the oysters, and the painting of Richie swept into it, the money sack swelled until it looked like it was about to explode. All at once, the dollar bills were plucked off of me. My shoes, stockings, and slip went next. I tried to hold onto a big pink piggy bank, but the suction was so strong I lost my grip and, headfirst, plunged toward the bulging, overstuffed bag...

The sound of a shrill siren interrupted my fall. It grew louder and louder, then abruptly stopped as an ambulance screeched to a halt outside the Prom Room door. Cautiously, I opened one eye. An out-of-focus Richie hovered over me, frantically waving a handful of hundred dollar bills in front of my face. "She's coming to!" he shouted at the crowd. "Stand back! Give her room to breathe!" "Room to breathe," I mumbled, and broke out in a fit of uncontrollable laughter. It seemed like the funniest thing in the whole world. I imagined myself propped in a large transparent tent, surrounded by doctors, attendants, and elaborate equipment. I imagined a caravan of trucks arriving with endless tanks of air shipped directly from the snowy peak of Mount Everest—pure intoxicating oxygen, the very best that money can buy.

SECRET AGENT GIRL

From the roof of the abandoned warehouse, Manhattan was a maze of glittering lights and gleaming neon. Not an unpleasant sight, I thought, as I peered over the edge of the building. But this was no night to relax and enjoy a beautiful view. I reminded myself that the matter at hand was one of great consequence. In fact, it was perhaps the most important assignment in my career as a female agent for U.N.C.L.E. (United Network Command of Law Enforcement). Agent 17225, to be precise, April Dancer. For years I'd poured every molecule of my being into combatting the deadly exploits of THRUSH, the secret organization with roots buried all over the world, just waiting to make its move for global domination. Few knew how close THRUSH was to achieving that evil goal. Somewhere inside this warehouse, which THRUSH was using as a temporary hideout, sat a black attaché case. This briefcase contained extremely confidential documents—highly specific top-secret data on nuclear warfare. The fate of the entire planet was at stake. My mission was to retrieve the briefcase and hand-carry it to the UN building, where an international conference was scheduled to take place at midnight. I looked at my wristwatch in the dim moonlight. It was already a quarter past ten. I would have to act fast.

I ripped open the hem of my red mini-skirt and extracted a thin synthetic rope, which scientists at U.N.C.L.E.'s Research Laboratory had recently perfected. A ton of concrete had been lifted with this super-fiber, without the slightest fray or tear. I knotted one end of the rope to a firm railing and tied the other end around my slim waist. I took a deep breath and leapt off the ledge, swinging out, high above the sparkling city, then back, right through an open window on the top floor. Whew! I landed upright, in the traditional jujitsu defense position. A large, burly character, who'd been snoozing on a fold-out cot against the wall, sprang to his feet. I recognized him immediately: Fritz Auschwitz (Code name: Rattler), one of THRUSH's most venomous undercover spies. He grunted and lunged towards me. With the blur of a comet, my right hand shot up and unhooked the cameo brooch fastened to my yellow roll-necked sweater. An oblong of brilliant onyx twinkled. I flung my hand at the man. With this gesture, a thick spray of inky fluid (released with the pressure of a forefinger on a concealed lever) saturated my assailant's eyes. He roared in surprise and pain, then thrashed forward, clawing at his contorted face. The blinding concoction had never had a more devastating effect. I now attacked him with expert hands, chopping savagely at his exposed neck. My final karate blow fell like the stroke of an ax. He groaned and sprawled facedown on the floor.

I brushed myself off and straightened my white half-domed patent leather cap. I stepped over the unconscious hulk and pressed my ear to the door. The electronic sound detector implanted in my dangling spiral earring indicated that it was safe to proceed. A darkened corridor stretched ahead. I reached inside my handbag and located a tube of lipstick which, when twisted counterclockwise, emitted an infrared ray that illuminated the hallway like a miniature flashlight. I advanced cautiously, my senses alert. Halfway down the hall, I picked up the murmur of several thick foreign accents. I knelt before a closed door and squinted into the keyhole. THRUSH, all right. Three of their most sinister agents clustered around a huge revolving green-and-blue translucent globe, on which scattered red lights flashed, designating the countries that had succumbed to THRUSH's control. I recognized each of the scoundrels from the dossiers I'd studied during my briefing session at U.N.C.L.E. Headquarters: the muscular Igor Smirnoff (Code name: Viper), the icy Erika von Häagen-Dazs (Code name: Asp), and the most lethal and cold-blooded of them all, the voluptuous Oolong Chong, alias China Doll (Code name: Cobra). I should have known that the diabolical China Doll had masterminded this clandestine affair. The mere sight of her sent shivers up and down my spine: painted lips and fingertips, twin fire-breathing dragons embroidered on the sleeves of her silk kimono, jade pagoda-shaped pendant, and two chopsticks which protruded like antennae from the peak of her coiled black hair. Snickering wickedly, she photographed the contents of the brief-case with a microcamera hidden in the beauty mark on her left cheek. There wasn't a moment to lose. I clutched my handbag (a .32 caliber bullet could be fired by triggering its metal clasp) and stretched back, bracing myself against the opposite wall. My strategy was simple: to force open the door by thrusting my full weight against it, thus taking the THRUSH agents unawares. Before I could execute my plan, however, a hard knee rocketed from nowhere, ramming into my stomach. The air shot out of my lungs. My eyes blurred with tears. I shook myself violently, trying to dissolve the waves of shock. I staggered, only to feel a brawny arm encircle my neck, jerking my head upward, while a sweet-smelling pad was held to my face. "Not zo fazt, Mees Danzer," muttered my unseen adversary. It was too late to retaliate. A tingling sensation swept through my entire body. Numbness paralyzed my limbs. Darkness whirled around me...

I came to in a tiny, four-walled cubicle. A bare light bulb glared overhead. Still groggy from the effects of the chloroform, I slowly assessed the seriousness of my predicament. I was propped in a wooden chair, my wrists bound firmly behind my back. A thick rope had also been wound around the ankles of my white patent-leather boots. Directly in front of me, a heavyset brute sat at an interrogation table examining the articles he'd spilled out of my handbag: silver cigarette case radio transmitter, miniature tape-recorder-compact with powder-puff microphone, Espionage Pink exploding nail polish (compound X-757), Foster Grant sunglasses equipped with self-focusing telescopic lenses, mascara, fountain pen, international passport, etc. Despite his elaborate disguise (beard, eyepatch and beret), I recognized my abductor: Jean-Claude de Sade (Code name: Fang), a notoriously sadistic double agent. I was well aware of his subversive tactics and tricks. While he ransacked my personal belongings, I lowered my head and, with my teeth, pulled a short plastic tube from the lapel of my red double-breasted sports jacket. This implement contained an opiate-coated dart capable of inducing complete unconsciousness for at least twenty-four hours. Puckering my lips, I pointed the tube at de Sade and blew into it. Bull's-eye! The dart lodged in the side of his broad neck, producing a trickle of blood. He moaned and crumpled forward like a limp rag doll.

I sprang into action. Rocking back and forth with increased velocity, I was able to propel myself to my feet. I bent down and rapidly sawed through the rope around my wrists by scraping it against the razor-sharp blades affixed to the inner-edges of my boot heels. I untied my ankles, jumped up, and scooped my dual-purpose devices into my purse. I paused to break open and sniff a small black capsule. Instant Wake-up, the Lab boys had labeled their discovery. Within seconds, I felt fully revived. I decided to freshen my makeup (a necessity for a girl agent on the go). As I applied a terrific new shade of lipstick, Undercover Red, I witnessed some unusual activity in the mirror of my compact. Behind me, a steel panel slid soundlessly across the wall, revealing a secret passage through which Smirnoff and von Häagen-Dazs slipped into the room, brandishing deadly weapons. Matter-of-factly, I snapped my handbag shut. Then, gripping it like a pistol, I spun around, showering my unsuspecting enemies with a barrage of "mercy" bullets—harmless, drug-filled pellets which acted immediately upon contact with the victim's skin. Stunned, they collapsed on top of each other.

I reloaded my handbag and forged ahead. Inside the passageway, a narrow staircase led me to the entrance of an exotic fortress: the face of an immense papier-mâché dragon adorned with fiery strips of red and gold foil. Its jaws stretched wide open and a thin crimson carpet unfurled from its mouth like a serpentine tongue. I entered the dragon. As I parted a beaded curtain, the heavy scent of incense assailed me. My body twinged with the sense of impending danger. Unwittingly, I'd stumbled into China Doll's private sanctum: a dimly lit den strewn with tasseled satin pillows and oriental rugs. On the wall, an ornate drapery depicted feudal warlords caught in the grip of mortal combat. I moved to the center of the chamber where, surrounded by a spiked iron railing, a circular pane of glass overlooked the luminous rotating globe. From this vantage point, China Doll could secretly scrutinize the goings-on in the room below. "Zo vee meet vonce more, Miz Dansor." China Doll had appeared from behind a black-and-gold folding screen. In one hand, she held the attaché case; in the other, a long black cigarette holder with a lit magenta Sobranie inserted in its tip. Her slanted eyes glowered with contempt. She tossed her head back and burst out in a fit of harsh laughter. The green light filtering through the glass spy-hole tinted her pale skin with a fiendish glow. She composed herself, set down the briefcase, and lifted the cigarette holder to her lips, as if to take a puff. Instead, she hurled it towards me like a spear. It flew across the room and penetrated my handbag, which I'd held up to shield myself. Instantaneously, my purse burst into flames. "Take zat, my pretty pretty," she cackled. Her underhanded move had rendered me defenseless. "Why you..." I grabbed a vase from a black lacquered pedestal. "Poot zat down!" she snapped. "Eat iz an anteek!" Deftly, I pitched it at her. She tried to catch the vase, but it slipped through her talonlike fingernails and shattered into a million pieces. "You vill pay for zis, Miz Dansor! My prizliz Ming!" Furiously, she plucked the chopsticks out of her hair and flung them in my direction. I ducked behind an engraved rosewood opium bed. The chopsticks whizzed past and exploded like firecrackers. Acid splattered everywhere, spitting and hissing as it ate through plaster, cushions, rugs and floorboards. Backing away, I bumped into an alabaster Buddha. "Be carefool, you little fool!" The statue smashed into fragments at my feet. "My Booda!" she wailed. Trembling with rage, China Doll grasped her jade pagoda pendant, ripped it off her neck, and threw it down. A cloud of chartreuse smoke billowed up and enveloped her. She reemerged on the other side of the room, clutching a bejeweled dagger. "AIEEE!!!" she shrieked, and charged towards me. Thinking fast, I dodged her attack and sprung behind her. As China Doll whirled around, I looked her square in the eye and landed a solid right cross to her jaw. Flailing her arms, she stumbled backwards, flipped over the iron railing, and crashed through the shimmering glass. For a moment, she hovered in midair, her kimono fluttering like the wings of a Japanese butterfly. Then she dropped straight down, impaling herself on the gold spire of the slowly revolving globe.

"I see I've arrived just in time." I turned to meet the grinning face of Mark Slate, my suave but tardy partner. He stared down at the impaled China Doll. "She's certainly made her mark on the world," he said glibly. He explained that he'd had trouble tracing the magnetic homing device in the buckle of my white patent-leather belt. I picked up the attaché case and took one last look at my defeated archenemy: her body draped on top of the spinning orb; her blood, like wet nail polish, spreading across oceans and continents, dripping below the equator, igniting sparks as it seeped into the motor at the base of the globe. Such a waste of beauty and brains, I thought. "C'mon, luv. The helicopter's waiting." Mark tugged me towards the fire escape. The China Doll Affair was over.

VII

POEM

The birds
of paradise
which Roy cut
for me from his
front yard sit
in the pink vase
on the floor and
point every
which way.
Carlos sits
in the green chair
nibbling his
salad. He keeps
eyeing the flower
closest to him.
Finally, he looks
over at me, gives
that mischievous
grin of his,
then pushes
it away.

LITTLE NOTHINGS

1

Carlos and I pick
up a few things at
the new Ralphs Giant
at Sunset and West-
ern and walk back to
his apartment. It's
his turn to cook, so
he's "in charge." Be-
tween dinner (fish,
broccoli, rice) and
dessert (chocolate ice
cream), we play a game
of Scrabble in his
bedroom. We spread
the board, letters
and letter holders
on the brown blanket
on Carlos' bed. I keep
score. After a while,
Carlos is ahead by
at least a hundred
points. It's almost
impossible for me
to form any words—
except for a "t",
I have all vowels.
Finally, I place
the "t" below
the "i" in Carlos'
last word ("milk"),
then draw another
vowel. I start
to exchange my
letters and Carlos
gives me a funny look.
"You can't do that."
"I have all vowels,"
I say, "You get to
trade them in when
you have all vowels."
"That's not in the

rules." "Yes it is."
I check, but can't
find it in the direc-
tions. "It's OK," he
says, "You can take
new ones." "Thank
you. You're very
generous." "But
you made up that rule."
He smiles at me. I
lean over and kiss his
neck. Then we push
the game aside and
lie back on the bed
and laugh and touch.

2

The phone rings
while I'm taking a nap.
"I just called to say
Hi," Carlos says.
He's about to make
dinner (beef
Stroganoff) for
his roommate Greg.
"What are you doing
after that?" I ask.
"I don't know."
"Do you want to
get together?"
"This is possible."
He says he'll call
me as soon
as they're through
eating. I tell
him I'm going
to take a long
bath. After we hang
up, I pull the phone
as close to the tub
as it will reach,
light a white candle
and soon inch in-

119

to the hot water,
The Bangles blasting
on the stereo
in the other room.

3

It's Friday night and
I'm "in charge." I
call the Domino's on
Hollywood Blvd. and
order a small pizza—
half with Carlos'
favorite toppings
(sausage and pepper-
oni) and half with
mine (black olives
and mushrooms).
Carlos arrives right
after the pizza's
delivered. "Did
you give a big tip?"
"I didn't give him
anything. I wasn't
sure if I was supposed
to." "You should have."
"I feel awful," I say
as I hand Carlos his
first slice. "Don't
let it ruin your
evening." "I won't.
But next time I'll
know." Joe knocks
on the door while
we're eating. He
and Christopher are
leaving for a week-
end in San Francisco.
"Well, is *he* here?"
"Oh. Yes. Come on in.
Joe, Carlos. Carlos,
Joe." They shake
hands. Joe inspects
our plates. "Pizza.

Yum." Christopher
calls Joe's name
from the bottom of
the stairs. "I gotta
go. Nice to meet you."
"You too." "Have a
nice time." "You too."
I close the door.
"That was Joe." "He
seems nice," Carlos says.
We finish eating, then
drive to Venice to hear
Dennis read. We hold
hands in the car, lis-
ten to one of my girl-
group tapes. It rains
on and off. After the
reading, we drive back
to my apartment. I make
dessert (cookies and milk)
and show Carlos a photo
album—pictures of
friends and of me in
my various phases:
overweight and thin,
on crutches, holding
cigarettes and beers,
with and without long
hair and a mustache.
Carlos likes my high
school graduation pic-
ture the best. "I was
stoned when it was taken,"
I tell him. Close-
mouthed, we kiss
and begin to undress
each other. "Shall we
get into bed?" "Yes."
I open the futon and
throw down sheets,
blankets and pillows,
then set the alarm so
we'll wake up in time
to watch "Pee-wee's
Playhouse." Carlos

lies on his stomach,
legs spread. I jump
on him. "You've been
pretty happy lately,"
he laughs. "Yes, I
have." "Would it be
presumptuous to think
it's because of me?"
"I don't think it
would be presumptuous
at all," I say as I
reach up to switch off
the lamp. "Don't," he
says, "I want to see
you." "OK." We make
love, cum at almost
the same time. We
lie still for a few
minutes, then wipe
ourselves with sep-
arate towels. "Now?"
"Now." I turn off
the light. We kiss
goodnight. And for
the first time since
we've been dating, we
fall asleep in each
other's arms.

FIVE HAIKU

October 20th

I was so surprised.
I'd never have thought you were
waiting, watching me.

*

Drive

One hand on the wheel
and the other, your right one,
gently clutching mine.

*

Dry Kisses

The safest kind. "I
could get used to kissing like
this," you said at first.

*

"Open Your Heart"

Madonna sang this
on the radio the day
yours suddenly closed.

*

What Lasts

How we opened up
and were affectionate for
one brief, sweet moment.

HAND OVER HEART

I look up at the clock.
It's time to go, so
I cover the typewriter
and calculator, lock my radio
in the file cabinet
and straighten my desk.
On the way out, I unplug
the Christmas tree lights.
I am rarely the last one
to leave the office.

Alone in the elevator,
I listen to a lilting
rendition of "Frosty
The Snowman." The door
slides open. Outside,
it's already dark. I say
good night to the guard
in the parking lot, wait
for my car to warm up.
It does and I drive off.

Halfway home,
I turn on the radio.
Madonna sings
her new hit, "Open
Your Heart." At
the same time, on
another station,
Cyndi Lauper sings
her latest song, "Change
Of Heart." Not that long
ago, it might have
been Brenda Lee
singing "Heart In Hand"
and Connie Francis
belting out any number
of her most popular
tunes: "My Heart
Has A Mind Of Its
Own," "Breakin' In
A Brand New Broken
Heart," "When

The Boy In Your Arms
(Is The Boy In Your
Heart)" or "Don't
Break The Heart
That Loves You."
I don't know why
I think about
such things.

I park the car
in the garage, walk
across the courtyard
and check the mailbox.
A few bills, ads,
Christmas cards
from friends I no
longer feel that
close to. No
messages on my
phone machine.

"I'm sorry,"
you said last
night. You seemed
sincere. Later,
I sat in my car
and cried. *Was it
love? I thought
it was love. I mean
it felt like love.*
It really did.

OSCAR NIGHT

When two-time Oscar winner
Olivia de Havilland comes
out in a red dress with see
-through sleeves to present
the award for Best Cinema-
tography, Christopher gasps:
"She's so affected! I just
love her!" Christopher, Joe
and I sit on the couch eating
pizza. "How splendid!" says
Olivia after she announces
the winner. An award or two
later, Janet (the cat) walks
into the room with a dead
bird in her mouth and deposits
it in front of the TV. "Oh
Janet!" Christopher sighs. He
picks up the bird and takes it
outside. "She does this at
least once a week," he says
when he returns, "I'm sure it
satisfies her somewhere deep
in her nature." Joe doesn't
miss a beat: "Just like Miss
de Havilland satisfies *you*?"

GOOD TIDINGS

Tonight, a hand-painted and
haloed cherub is watching
over you as you drift off.
It is the same angel that
inhabits the candle's shadows,
the spirit that dwells
in your glass of warm milk.
It is also the protector
of good art and the speaker
of all romance languages,
as well as the guardian of
your dreams and little wishes,
and the keeper of each dark
secret you swore you would
take to the grave, but which
you have given up this time
around—your second and final
chance. So turn away from
the light. Sleep. Let go
of every unknown answer and
explanation. When you wake,
you will own your life.

BOOKS AVAILABLE FROM AMETHYST PRESS

IDOLS
By Dennis Cooper $8.95
BEDROOMS HAVE WINDOWS
By Kevin Killian $9.95
HORSE AND OTHER STORIES
By Bo Huston $8.95
MUSIC I NEVER DREAMED OF
By John Gilgun $9.95
THE BLACK MARBLE POOL
By Stan Leventhal $8.95
THE BURIED BODY
By Mark Ameen $10.95
THIS EVERY NIGHT
By Patrick Moore $8.95
REMEMBER ME
By Bo Huston $9.95
HAND OVER HEART
By David Trinidad $9.95

These books are available from your favorite bookseller or by mail from:

Amethyst Press
6 West 32nd Street
Penthouse
New York, NY 10001-3808

Add $2.00 postage and handling for one book. For more than one book add an additional fifty cents per book. New York State residents please add appropriate sales tax. US currency only. Personal checks and money orders please. To order by Credit Card: **1-800-331-4427**